Lamplight Collection of Modern Art

Redon, Seurat and the Symbolists

Lamplight Publishing, Inc.
New York, New York

PUBLISHED IN THE UNITED STATES OF AMERICA IN 1975
by Lamplight Publishing, Inc., N.Y. 10016

First published in the series "Mensili d'Arte" Copyright © 1967
by Fratelli Fabbri Editori, Milan, Italy

Illustrations Copyright © 1970 by Fratelli Fabbri Editori, Milan,
Italy on the American Edition.

ALL RIGHTS RESERVED, PRINTED IN ITALY

Library of Congress Catalog Card Number: 70-1066-57
SBN 0-88308-012-5

The Origins of Symbolism

Symbolism began as a literary movement in France in the 1880s and 1890s. The form of expression that we now call Symbolism appeared first in poetry but soon spread to music and to art, where it led to completely novel modes of creativity. Before we turn to our brief history of the Symbolist movement in painting, we must place it in context by looking at its literary origins.

Literary Symbolism resulted from the efforts of a small group of French poets to liberate themselves from the philosophies that had dominated letters and art throughout most of the nineteenth century. The Symbolists were moved by the urge to find a fresh way of expressing ultimate reality. In their search and experiments, the Symbolist poets anticipated many of the themes and motifs that were to characterize the literature and art of the twentieth century.

Although the Symbolists sought for "something new," they could not entirely free themselves from nineteenth-century philosophies and ideas. They formed their concepts, however, by bringing together existent opposing ideas in an important new "synthesis." Thus Idealism and Naturalism, which in the early years of the nineteenth century had been seen as opposites, were joined — or *synthesized* — by the Symbolists to yield new and deeper meaning. In a sense, then, Symbolism was a movement, first in literature and later in art, in which a creative originality drew upon its sources but went beyond previous ideas into a new reality. Looking back, we can see that while the Symbolists did not belong to the mainstream of the thought of their century, they were nevertheless unable to make a clean break with its traditions.

Although Symbolism began with a small group of French poets, we must understand that the movement was not consciously invented and developed entirely by a group of associates working together at one time. Rather, the Symbolist movement grew over a period of forty years as each man in turn made his contribution. The most influential of all was the poet Charles Baudelaire. He is looked upon by many as the first and possibly the greatest of all the Symbolist poets. Yet Baudelaire died in 1867, nearly twenty years before the central concepts of the movement were organized and given the name by which we now identify them.

Baudelaire was followed by the poets Paul Verlaine, Stéphane Mallarmé, and Arthur Rimbaud, all of whom were influenced by him. Their common bond was the search for worldly meaning in unworldly imagination. Although these three are known as Symbolists, it was left to a later generation of poets born around 1860 to codify the Symbolist doctrines in a series of polemic statements or *manifestos* that began to appear in 1886. Among the group were the minor poets Jean Moréas, Gustave Kahn, René Ghil, and Charles Morice.

The themes and techniques that were later to form a Symbolist doctrine were present in the works of Baudelaire, Verlaine, Mallarmé, and Rimbaud, but we must note that their work also contained other themes and elements. The great contribution of these men was that they realized the possibilities of an art dominated by imagination and, in so doing, broke away from the tradition of nineteenth-century literature.

It often happens that the creators of new movements in literature or art are so engrossed in the act of creation that they neglect to explain their insights. It was left to the minor poets—Moréas, Kahn, Ghil, and others—to find and express the Symbolist doctrines implicit in the writings of Baudelaire, Verlaine, Mallarmé, and Rimbaud. The younger men interpreted the movement and placed it in historic context.

Symbolism and Synthesis

Moréas was the first to attempt to formulate the Symbolist doctrine. In an article, or rather a manifesto, that appeared in 1886, Moréas clearly saw the central motif of Symbolism as a fusion of Naturalism and Idealism, which until then had been regarded as antithetical. According to Moréas, the search for reconciliation modified the meanings of Naturalism and Idealism to yield a new concept. As he put it, "Symbolistic poetry endows the Idea with form, but in such a way that form does not become an end in itself, but is subordinated to the Idea it seeks to express. The Idea, on the other hand, must not appear to be completely independent of the elements of form that give it reality, for the essential character of Symbolist art consists of avoiding the error of giving independent existence to the Idea."

Gustave Kahn expanded the theory by emphasizing that one should not concentrate only on the study of "real" life, as the Naturalists had done, but take everything into consideration, even dreams and the wildest concepts of the imagination. The ideas of Kahn were taken a step further by Charles Morice, who was to give the most complete exposition of the Symbolist doctrines.

The strength of Morice's theory lay in its being a systematic synthesis of elements from antithetical philosophies, that is, Naturalism and Idealism. This synthesis, as earlier shown, is the dominant characteristic of Symbolism. In Morice's statement of the Symbolist view, there is agreement between the spirit and the senses: The sensual (or physical) elements tend to become ethereal and the spiritual elements tend to become relatively concrete and tangible. According to Morice, Symbolism found a way to reconcile the opposing elements of truth and beauty, faith and reason, science and art. This reconciliation or "synthesis" was proclaimed by Morice to be the Symbolist banner heralding rejection of the "analytical" attitude that had dominated the preceding age. He wrote: "Synthesis returns the spirit to its true country.... Synthesis in art is the joyous dream of beautiful truth...a fruitful pact of alliance between natural science and metaphysics."

During the 1880s Symbolist thought was greatly influenced by a pseudoscientist and student of aesthetics, Charles Henry. He seemed to be able to confirm the concept that synthesis was indeed possible between science and metaphysics and between physical manifestations of nature and the spirit or Ideal. Henry's name was linked to many aspects of Symbolist painting, and he was often quoted by both artists and critics. In fact, Henry maintained that it was possible to establish by experiment an exact equivalence between certain phenomena and certain states of mind or spirit. For example, Henry sought to identify which actions were capable of giving pleasure and then to measure the degree of pleasure they evoked. He thought it possible to identify how colors act upon our feelings to produce joy or sadness. In his desire to confirm the

Symbolist concept of synthesis by experimental research, Henry took the Baudelairian doctrine of "correspondences" directly to the laboratory.

Symbolism and Idealism

It is possible to say with some confidence that Symbolism's main purpose was thus to reconcile and synthesize the sensuous and the spiritual. There were, however, some theorists and critics who emphasized the spirit, or Ideal, but are still to be counted among the Symbolists. They were, perhaps, overreacting against Naturalism. One such writer was Joris Karl Huysmans. He started his career as a follower of Zola toward the end of the 1870s. Huysmans broke with Zola, however, in his novel *A Rebours* (1884). The book caused a scandal at the time. Its main character is a nobleman, Des Esseintes, created as the archetype of turn-of-the-century aestheticism. In the novel this character is motivated by a constant concern to model his life on an excessively refined and bizarre pattern of behavior that clashed with the normal everyday life preferred by the Naturalist writers. Notable among Des Esseintes' many eccentricities was the collecting of paintings that were obviously inspired by a taste completely counter to the Naturalism of the 1870s. Huysmans was thus the first novelist to develop a character who expressed the new feelings of the times.

Public discussion of the novel developed into violent arguments between the Naturalists and those obstinately opposed to Naturalism, who tried to go beyond it to Symbolism. Attention was also focused on the artists Gustave Moreau, Rodolphe Bresdin, Odilon Redon, and Pierre Puvis de Chavannes, who are mentioned by name in Huysmans' work. These men are thought of today as the fathers of Symbolist painting. A close examination, however, reveals that their contributions to the movement were not of the same order. Moreau, Puvis de Chavannes, and Bresdin should be called precursors of Symbolism, while Redon participated fully in the movement.

The Precursors of Symbolist Painting

Gustave Moreau and Pierre Puvis de Chavannes were both born in the 1820s. Although quite different from each other, both are known as "Idealists." They shared an opposition to the liberties taken with history common among the Romantics and to the Naturalist themes and genre paintings of other artists. Rather than follow either of these paths, Moreau and Puvis de Chavannes painted a world remote from modern times, filled with heroes and primitive figures lost in a retrospective dream. This attempt to dampen the enthusiasm of the Romantics and oppose the Naturalist trend found its counterpart in other movements taking place in Europe during the middle nineteenth century. In both Pre-Raphaelite England and the Germany of Böcklin and von Marées we find a similarity of interest and thinking to the work in France.

Obviously, despite a common purpose, each artist developed a distinctive style. Moreau, for example, is noted for his lack of emotion. His paintings are characterized by their smooth, rounded, marblelike figures finished with meticulous detail and by an abundance of decorative elements. The work of Puvis de Chavannes is much sweeter and often somewhat melancholy; in it we find the warm Mediterranean atmosphere reminiscent of the classical canvases of Nicolas Poussin. But when considering the Symbolist movement, we are interested in those aspects of the approach of Moreau and Puvis de Chavannes to make new use of design and of heavy contours, for the later Symbolists were to place great emphasis on these elements.

The later Symbolists were also indebted to these artists for having upheld the beautiful and the elegant and for preserving a nobility of form at a time when these concepts seemed to have been swept away by the emphasis on being true to nature. But, on the other hand, the most ardent of the succeeding generation of Symbolists certainly realized that Moreau and Puvis de Chavannes had perhaps overreacted. For on their canvases the two pre-Symbolists had expressed beauty analytically rather than suggesting it by the use of symbolic nuances.

Odilon Redon

The case of Odilon Redon, the last and youngest artist mentioned by Huysmans, is quite different. The very circumstances of his life seem to suggest that he was a living example of the synthesis of opposing forces characteristic of Symbolism. Redon was influenced in his early period by Bresdin and especially by Moreau. They passed on to Redon the cult of the beautiful and an appreciation of classic forms. He was also influenced by Camille Corot, one of the most famous and enduring masters of Naturalism. Another important factor was that Redon was born in 1840, which made him a contemporary of Monet and other Impressionists, with whom, incidentally, he maintained excellent relations—he appeared in at least one of their annual exhibits. In common with the Impressionists, Redon was a close and diligent student of nature. He even made a detailed study of botany. His artist's eye was aware of all the brightness and color of sun-warmed air. Redon's attitude was quite different from the narrow, morbid outlook expressed in Moreau's canvases or from the kind of Naturalism that Puvis de Chavannes represented in his murals.

If nature was the starting point for Redon, it was not—as it was with the Impressionists—a goal that fulfilled and satisfied his artistic quest. Nature, in fact, left Redon unsatisfied. His tendency was to focus on nature as a beginning, or point of departure, and then to isolate himself from a natural context, emphasizing other dimensions that transform the natural into magic and enigma. Redon soon tired of the present and perceptible world, to become interested in seeking both its origins and its future. In his painting he suggests that the visible is not everything; just beyond the seen is the hint of a mysterious unseen. Redon suggested this technically by alternating "finished" and "unfinished" areas in his paintings, to render the objects in them vague and elusive.

Redon achieved his nuances in a smooth and apparently effortless manner, a result of his exclusive dedication to drawing and illustration during the early and middle years of his career, when he produced many series of charcoal drawings and lithographs. It is in the lithographic album of 1879, *Dans le Rêve* (The Dream), that the first obvious expression of Symbolist art is to be found. (This was several years before Moréas and the young poets had formulated their manifestos.) Even the title of his collection is significant, for the lithographs deal with the revenge that dreams take on real life. To Redon dreams were not alien to life itself, but subtly linked to it. His reveries are dreams that manage to insert their mysterious logic into the heart of the most real experiences of daily life, to bestow upon them a resonance and added meaning. But for Redon, painting was not a matter merely of depicting a universe filled with hideous and absurd nightmares. Rather, the figments of his dream world, although horrible and often frightening to the beholder, had their meaning in the enrichment of life itself. He had found his synthesis of the spirit and the material.

In his later years Redon illustrated masterpieces of visionary and horror literature, such as Poe's tales and Flaubert's *La Tentation de Saint Antoine*. But he never allowed himself to be carried away by the horror of the tales, always managing to distinguish between the traumatic and brutal impact of evil and the subtle evocation of a vague, alluring unknown.

Even more successful than these illustrations were a series of drawings based on Darwin's theory of evolution, which was much in vogue in Redon's time and to which he dedicated his cycle, *Les Origines*. It was clear to Redon that nature poses dramatic questions concerning its origin and its ultimate destiny, confronting the observer with fascinating enigmas. Thus, through his interest in nature, Redon expressed in his art the essence of Symbolism—the quest for meaning in the slow and gradual process of seeking synthesis between the certain and the uncertain, between physics and metaphysics.

The early work of Redon, far in advance of its time, was a statement in black and white. Redon's work, for this reason, attracted admirers who were particularly inclined toward satanism and perversion and who believed they had found a perfect ally in Redon. They did not understand that the great dark areas in his lithographs were not intrinsic signs of inner desperation, nor evocations of evil, but merely another suitable technique used to achieve his poetic nuances.

In the 1890s Redon developed a highly chromatic style and began to produce paintings in an intensely sensuous mood. Those who had understood the true inspiration of Redon's "black" lithographs were not surprised to see his new work. In the new paintings light and elusive colors form halos; nature explodes in vivid particles, fragmenting itself in a haze of insects seeking out multihued flowers. Thus out of dissolution (the antithetical struggle) emerges new form (synthesis), expressed as a symbol.

Eugène Carrière

Eugène Carrière, although much more limited and less imaginative, had a similar outlook to that of Redon. He too was a pioneer of the new nonfinite art of nuances. His technique, however, never developed quite to the point where his attempts to portray inner meaning equaled the demands of his ambitious undertakings—his vision exceeded his skill. It is also evident that Carrière did not have the intellect or the insight of Redon. Although he attempted many promising experiments in his treatment of groups of people, individual figures, and portraits, his paintings have a rather academic appearance. But Carrière is significant in the growth of the Symbolist idea, and it is in this respect that his work is of interest.

Symbolism and the Divisionism of Seurat

The highly original work of Georges Seurat gave great impetus to the evolution of Symbolistic painting between 1880 and 1890. At the outset of his career,

Seurat seemed to be attracted both by nature and the Impressionist movement. In his early work, he copied the Impressionists' optical brightness and brushstrokes. This drew him away from the Symbolist concept of "synthesis," but the techniques he developed were to prove in a superb fashion how Symbolism could be reached through fidelity to reality and a scientific approach. As modern theoretical science has clearly shown, close observation of nature leads ultimately to uncertainty, where the elusive elements of reality can be grasped only intellectually.

In a long series of designs and sketches, we can see how Seurat seemed driven to rationalize the Impressionist techniques, that is, to preserve the use of color but to supplant spontaneity with form and order. This search took Seurat to the point where he was forced to abandon the felicitous unity of color and form that the Impressionists had struggled to perfect. In Impressionist paintings, every brushstroke is a rendering both of light and of a recognizable object at the same time. A branch, the roof of a house, an animal—indeed, every part of the work— has its particular characteristics, which allow the observer to recognize it quickly —to receive the "impression" of the moment.

In Seurat's canvases, what happens instead is that nature loses its readily decipherable aspect. It is not possible to observe in a single glance what the artist wants us to see. Instead, through the use of dots and dashes of color equal to each other in value, the subject is transformed into a vibration that no longer represents a familiar object. Seurat made use of this energy-charged dance of light and color, and of the phenomena of radiation, reflection, and contrast, to define the classic solidity of form in a new way. In a sense, Seurat was approaching in the field of art the same problems that scientists had been studying in their investigations of light and color, and he turned to their treatises for information. From his studies of color and light came an important theory, which he called "chromo-luminosity." Today this theory is better known as Neo-Impressionism or Divisionism.

This fusion of light and color was used in Seurat's painting *Bathing at Asnières* (1883–84), which was rejected by the official Salon in 1884 but was later shown with success in avant-garde circles and with the Independents group. Despite the fact that when he painted *Bathing at Asnières*, Seurat was still far from utilizing in full depth all the principles of Divisionism, he attracted supporters to the cause. The most prominent of the early converts was Paul Signac, who became the official theorist of the movement. Later there followed Albert Dubois-Pillet, Charles Angrand, Henri-Edmond Cross, and even a leading painter of the preceding generation, Camille Pissarro.

At first sight Divisionism appears to be an attempt to capture on canvas the truth of the optical fact. But when carried to its extreme limits, the technique fragments the norms of pictorial representation and transforms the "truth" into fluctuating and amorphous stipplings of color, which no longer show the immediate aspects of nature. Instead, the observer feels that something more profound and more solid has emerged. Because the brushstroke was looked upon with disfavor, since it gave paintings a uniform quality, a new approach was called for. Seurat now reintroduced to his work a technique that had been deliberately abandoned by the Impressionists: He returned to the use of schematic contours and carefully harmonized shapes. But Seurat's shapes and contours were treated so that they could be represented by the chromatic dots of the Divisionist school. In his work shapes and contours were divested of inessential ornaments and composed of undulating, supple rhythms that took on form among the myriad points of color.

This sinuous modulation of shape can be clearly seen in Seurat's well-known painting *A Sunday Afternoon on the Island of La Grande-Jatte* (1884–86). In this painting the artist beautifully harmonized the contours and shapes, while building them up of nothing more than points of paint to suggest line and mass. Principles of design that are apparently magical take over everyday themes to manifest the mysterious harmony of the universe, in which color and light are as one with matter and form.

Seurat's next experiments extended these characteristics and emphasized the values of line and composition. In a sense, Seurat had come to Impressionist Naturalism by a new route. It is not surprising that at this time he became a devoted follower of Charles Henry, whose rigorously calculated system of "correspondences" led Seurat to experiment with the theories on canvas. Henry believed that the position and angle of a figure could produce happiness, exaltation, or depression in the spectator; colors, too, serve a function of mental suggestion.

The use made by Seurat of Henry's mixture of science and mysticism can be seen in the last paintings by the young artist made toward the end of the 1880s. Whether in *La Parade* (Plate 13), in *Le Chahut* (Plate 15), or in *The Circus* (Plate 14), the human shapes appear with increasingly sharp definition. They move — or appear to move — with agile and sinuous movements; they seem to twist and dart. The chromatic dots, which by now have become extremely fine, are similar to a dusting of iron filings that, placed near the poles of a magnet, bring into view the otherwise invisible lines of force and so define the magnetic field. So, by analogy, were Seurat's points of color organized and oriented by the strength of his subjects. As we view one of his paintings, we become aware of what seem to be intense charges of energy on the coattails of the male dancers or on the slender shoulders of the female dancers, which give them a spinning, spiral movement. There is an invisible but powerful force in Seurat's work that makes each part of the canvas seem to flower, as if it were a unique living organism.

Paul Gauguin

Of all artists, the one most closely associated with the Symbolist movement is neither Redon nor Seurat, but Paul Gauguin. Gauguin's fame does not necessarily imply that his work was artistically superior to that of Redon or Seurat. In evaluating Gauguin, we must recognize that artistic merit is not the only criterion of fame and that some of his celebrity comes from the publicity given to his life. In many ways, Gauguin's struggle to escape from the artificial and complex life of late-nineteenth-century Europe and his search for freedom of spirit exemplify the values the Symbolists sought in art.

Born in 1848, Paul Gauguin was too young to be a part of the Impressionist generation, but too old to join freely in the artistic life of the Symbolists. The drama of Gauguin is that of a man who, no longer satisfied with what his times have to offer, searches for a different situation, which he vaguely perceives but cannot clearly define. The life and career of Gauguin were complicated because although his character was strong and persevering, his development of a vision of art was both erratic and unsure. He lacked the clarity of insight that characterized Redon and Seurat.

Throughout his career Gauguin moved with compulsive excitement, driven by a tremendous desire to "do" and to look for something "new." But in addition to his lack of direction, certain circumstances in Gauguin's life made him for some time a dilettante, or "Sunday painter." In the 1870s he became a wealthy broker, for whom painting was only a hobby, although he practiced it with intelligence and devotion. Because of his wealth and great interest in painting, he became friendly with Monet, Pissarro, Degas, and Cézanne and could help them by buying some of their work.

Gauguin's bourgeois roots contributed to the relative delay in the development of his artistic career and were the probable cause, in his reaction against them, of his dramatic clash with the "nice" middle-class values of the time. He came to personify the avant-garde artist's protest against society.

Early in his career, Gauguin was influenced by the Impressionist Camille Pissarro, whose subject matter and deliberate brushstroke technique were useful models for the inexperienced Gauguin, who also worked slowly and deliberately in contrast with the swift execution of the Impressionists. Thus Gauguin's slower rate of working and more careful construction found an example in Pissarro. The second influence on Gauguin was Cézanne, the product of a school very similar to that of Pissarro, with whom he had briefly studied. Cézanne also emphasized a deliberate and extended brushstroke. This influence did not altogether benefit Gauguin's art. It is true that he learned a fundamental lesson in synthesis from Cézanne, but with this he also developed a love of plasticity, which became a distraction in working out his own style.

By this time Gauguin had abandoned his family and his position in a stockbroker's office to begin a feverish, restless existence that often took him away from Paris in search of less expensive places to live. A brief stay in Brittany, at Pont-Aven, where he went in 1886, seemed to offer him several advantages. Along with economic benefits there were other more subtle ones: the nobility and the festive spirit of the local folklore and, above all, the beautiful regional costumes, which were irresistibly charming to a generation jaded by modern life in a big city.

Gauguin did not break with the Naturalist tradition at Pont-Aven. Although the canvases he painted of shepherdesses, peasants, farms, and flocks hint at his later style, descriptive details were still all-important and the concept of synthesis was not developed. Gauguin did not, in fact, head in the direction of synthesis until 1887, when he went to Panama and Martinique with his colleague Charles Laval and abandoned himself to the exotic life of the warm Caribbean. The views of tropical landscapes and expanse of ocean inspired him to paint with a sense of unity. But in general the change of scenery did not free him or contribute to his artistic growth. It was only through contact with the avant-garde in Paris that he could hope to find the key to developing his talent. But even after his return to Paris in early 1888, the city did not seem to offer him much: He received only the devoted and generous hospitality of his friend and colleague Jacob Meyer de Haan.

The School of Pont-Aven

Later that year Gauguin returned to Pont-Aven. It was at this time that he renewed and strengthened his association with a young and promising artist,

Emile Bernard. Despite the difference in their ages, both men were at the point of artistic maturity where each could gain and grow from their association. From a technical and stylistic viewpoint, Bernard was without doubt more advanced than his colleague Gauguin. His youth permitted the kind of radical solution that Gauguin would not have attempted on his own, for the influence of Pissarro and Cézanne was still very strong. Bernard had not, however, achieved his technical excellence entirely on his own. He had been much influenced by another young man, Louis Anquetin. Anquetin was, perhaps, the prime mover in the trend established by these three men, which became known as the School of Pont-Aven.

At this point we should look backward to 1886, the year in which some of the leading figures in future events were students at a private art school held in the studio of Cormon. Among the group at Cormon's studio were Toulouse-Lautrec, who had—forsaking his aristocratic background—recently taken up painting full-time in preference to legal training; van Gogh, who had just arrived in Paris, and Anquetin. This school was a meeting place for the men and ideas that had such important influence on the Symbolist movement.

The Cloisonnistes

Anquetin and Bernard had been briefly intrigued by the Divisionism of Seurat, but later abruptly dropped it. Together they initiated an important style of the Symbolist movement: *Cloisonnisme*—a technique in which color is laid down within sharply defined areas, or *cloisons*. (The term was derived from the system of enamel-making called cloisonné, where the molten enamels are poured into compartments cleanly divided by metal wires.) As the critic Dujardin said with regard to some of Anquetin's paintings: "Cloisonnisme is characterized by internal boundaries within which color is spread flatly and compactly in a fashion exactly opposite to the fractionalized art of the Divisionist painters." To the present-day viewer, however, the fluid contours of the cloisonné color areas do not appear too different from the sinuous figures of Seurat, making us realize that these techniques had more in common than their protagonists believed.

Although Anquetin had already achieved some success with his *Seminatore*, it was only in 1889 that his strength became apparent in a daring composition of particularly curved, undulating forms, *Pont Neuf in Paris* (Plate 55). Bernard, on the other hand, had to his credit such Symbolist works as *Girl with a Goose* and *Jug of Honey*. And after his meeting with Gauguin at Pont-Aven, Bernard quickly saw that he could use the folklore and legendary heritage of Brittany in a subtle, almost neo-Gothic vein that was extremely elegant.

Bernard's style was more advanced than that of his older colleague, and Gauguin, realizing that Cloisonnisme was the breakthrough he had been seeking for so long, began working in this new technique with strength and authority. Cloisonnisme would have had little impact but for Gauguin's use of it. In fact, Bernard retreated from experimentation with cloisonné technique and returned to a traditional and academic style.

Gauguin, on the other hand, began to strengthen this fragile technique, developing forceful, and sometimes even coarse and violent, contours that excited many artists. Also, perhaps because of his long search for a new and advanced style, Gauguin was more aware of the beauty and freedom that it gave to painting. Although Cézanne's work remained an important influence, Gauguin stayed with the severity of synthesis and spent the last ten fruitful years of his life trying to promote his ideas.

The year 1889 was a high point for Gauguin and marks the culmination of his experimentation with technique. Important paintings of that year are *The Yellow Christ* (Plate 18), *Calvary*, and *Christ in the Garden of Olives* (in which his own self-portrait stands for Christ). The mystic essence of these paintings is evident from their titles. Gauguin, however, used evangelical and biblical themes more in a search for self-insight than from true religious conviction. The representation of these traditional subjects helped Gauguin find a simplicity of line and led him to a world free of and beyond time, extraneous to the disturbing aspects of modern life. The Naturalist elements were now completely excluded from Gauguin's style, and his figures were drawn on one plane, in a rendering characterized by marked contours and intense, almost pure colors laid down in flat, well-defined areas. Symbolism had now found its style.

The Formulation of Synthesis

In 1889 the artists of the School of Pont-Aven felt that both they and the time were ready for an exhibition of their new work. Because of the unorthodox, iconoclastic, and experimental nature of their paintings, the exhibit was without official backing—in fact, semiclandestine. It was held at the Café Volpini, chosen for its location close to the great Universal Exhibition in Paris. In those years Impressionism was making the headlines and attracting the public, so it was thought necessary to call this controversial exhibit an "Impressionist Show." However, the organizers added as a subtitle to the catalog the flexible label of "synthesis." The most important exhibitors were Gauguin and Bernard, but experimental works by Laval, Emile Schuffenecker, Léon Fauché, Daniel de Monfreid, Louis Roy, and Anquetin were also included.

The leaning of the Pont-Aven School toward synthesis became much more evident when a precise theory was formulated. It was around this time that a young writer, Albert Aurier, became friendly with Gauguin, the central figure of the movement, and soon after with Charles Morice. Daily discussions became their practice, and as a result of these meetings Aurier wrote a "doctrinal letter" on the new art. In this memorable article he stated that art of the new experimental epoch had to be an art of "ideation" rather than of "idealism," because, he said, "art should not describe the idea but rather suggest it and express it in an abbreviated form." Aurier wrote that "this mode of suggestion makes art Symbolistic and synthetic—the symbols are condensed and reduced to allow the least possible error. In this way the art becomes subjective—the object portrayed will never be considered as such, but only as an indication of an idea perceived by the subject." Finally, Aurier stated, "art must be decorative. Truly decorative painting, as understood by the Greeks, the Egyptians, and the primitive painters, is above all else a manifestation of the subjective, synthetic, Symbolist, and conceptual in art."

Gauguin in Tahiti

A year before the Café Volpini exhibit and the publication of the Aurier theory on the Symbolist movement, Gauguin went to the south of France at van Gogh's invitation. Van Gogh, who had been an admirer and friend of Gauguin for some time, was now living at Arles, in Provence. The brief visit—so important for the Dutch artist—did little to allay Gauguin's restlessness. His need for escape was no longer satisfied by the narrow life and homespun exoticism shared with friends in Brittany and Provence. The lure of the tropics was strong, and in 1891 he traveled to the island of Tahiti in the South Pacific. There, in a primitive location away from the restrictions and conventions of European life, Gauguin found a measure of contentment. But because of poor health, he came back to France, only to return to Tahiti a few years later. In 1901 he went on to the Marquesas Islands, where he died in 1903 of the effects of disease and poverty.

How can we objectively evaluate the Tahitian period? We must start by mentioning once again the importance of his time in Brittany, since it was there that Gauguin developed his mastery of the synthetic style. The biblical tradition and Breton folklore were a greater source of inspiration than anything he saw in Tahiti. We may ask whether Gauguin actually saw nature and the true aspects of Oceania, or whether he used the lush tropical environment as a substitute for the visions he had already conceived in France.

Although Gauguin's Tahitian paintings are the most widely known, it does not seem that the time he spent in the islands can be considered the determining factor in his career. Rather, these last years were an extension and consolidation of the concepts and techniques he had previously worked out at the cost of much anguish. Perhaps, in the final analysis, we should view Gauguin's Tahitian period as the systematic development of a plan to find and portray the essence of man stripped of all "modern" sophistication and brought back into direct contact with the fundamental and mysterious events of life and death, of love and religion. Gauguin wished to paint a kind of primordial humanity whose every gesture is valued not merely for its own sake, but for what it represents as a generalized, symbolic, imperishable distillation of thousands of other similar gestures made by individuals who perish. To confirm this, it is enough to perceive that the famous painting *Where do we come from? What are we? Where are we going?* (Plate 23) represents, in a sense, the Tahitian cycle. The title alone shows the Symbolist taste for deep, elusive questions.

Vincent van Gogh

The name of Vincent van Gogh has already appeared in reference to the time when he attended Cormon's studio in Paris, and again in reference to his stay in Provence, where he experienced a vision of art vastly different from that of Gauguin. Van Gogh did not begin painting until he was nearly thirty, after he had had difficult and unhappy experiences in his attempts to enter the ministry and in love. The Dutch artist was naturally outgoing, especially in his relationships with other painters, although they did not always reciprocate. He felt great enthusiasm for those in the avant-garde movement and spent a great deal of time talking with and learning from them. Despite his friendliness, van Gogh remained an isolated figure. Separated from the Symbolist school by his need to develop a personal, unmistakable art, van Gogh never led a movement, nor did he become identified with any of the various doctrines.

The gulf between the approach to art of van Gogh and that of Gauguin or Seurat is vast. The latter artists had abandoned the strictly optical Impressionist art in which telling a story or emphasizing moral or emotional values had been discarded in favor of an overriding emphasis on light and chromatic vibration. Instead, as we have seen, the Symbolists undervalued light and color vibrancy and reintroduced the concept of line and contour to portray a spiritual vision.

Van Gogh, on the other hand, emerged from the Nordic tradition of popular, sentimental Naturalism, emotion-laden and emphasizing human suffering. His empathy with the poor can be seen in his portrayals of miners and peasants (*The Potato Eaters*—Plate 26). This "Nordic" Naturalism—which had no influence on Impressionism—used the dull and earthy colors resulting from a climate with little bright sunlight. But as van Gogh developed under the Impressionist influence, he lightened his palette and illuminated the atmosphere of his paintings with the brightness of the Mediterranean sun, bringing to his canvases the intense glitter of colors in their purest state.

It is evident, then, that in the art of van Gogh an important new thematic change took place as his art passed from Symbolism on a social level—that is, from an intense feeling for the misfortunes of laborers and peasants—to Symbolism on a universal level. Van Gogh's characteristic style developed into a poignant personal Symbolism, as the inspiration he received from the blinding sun and exuberant landscapes of Provence finally only increased his nervous and mental tension.

From a study of van Gogh's paintings it is possible to determine when he could accept advice or teaching and when he rejected guidance in favor of his own way. At the beginning of his stay in Paris, van Gogh was interested in the Divisionist movement and from this learned to brighten his palette. He could not, however, accept the Divisionists' blithe experiments with the representation of nature. He was also influenced by Bernard and Gauguin, who were then working with Cloisonnisme; at this time he also studied Japanese prints. The technique of Cloisonnisme was too confining for van Gogh who, rather than adopt this method, augmented the thickness of his pigments and spread them directly from the tube. Gauguin could not forgive him for this, and they had many impassioned arguments when they were together in Arles in 1888.

Gauguin's failure to understand his friend's need to develop his own style was one of the causes leading to their estrangement. Van Gogh's increasing anguish and mental instability at this time are apparent in his work. His inner turmoil is expressed in the thick, swirling paint and brilliant color. After a final quarrel with Gauguin, van Gogh had his first attack of madness and never fully recovered his mental equilibrium. He spent the last months of his life in an asylum at Saint-Rémy and then under medical supervision at Auvers-sur-Oise, where he committed suicide in July, 1890. Vincent van Gogh's tragic life and brilliant canvases have made him almost legendary. Although he was not a leader, nor a member, of any of the movements of the nineteenth century, he learned from all of them, developing an individual style that makes him one of the foremost painters of his time.

The drive that ultimately led van Gogh to self-destruction also led to the destruction in his work of preexisting concepts of pictorial structure. He had absorbed the lessons of Impressionism and had experimented with the technique of painting in dots and in short strokes laid side by side to bring brilliance into the canvas. But in his hands the method was transformed into something quite different from the intention of the Impressionists. Van Gogh used brushstrokes not only to break up color, but to express his own excitement. In effect, the stroke in itself became an essential element of the painting as this took shape. His curving strokes express ferment even within the well-defined contours of sunflowers, fields, and trees. No artist before him had used the brush with such consistent power or to such effect.

As we have noted, van Gogh's art was both incandescent and personal. He painted in a frenzy of creation, facing reality as a barrier to be broken down. Painting and living became one. He wrote, "Instead of trying to render exactly what I see before me, I use color more arbitrarily in order to express myself strongly."

The Nabis

During the 1880s, another group of young artists was working together at the Julian Academy in Paris. The leader of the students was Paul Sérusier, who had stayed in Pont-Aven, where he had come under the influence of Gauguin. Then in his twenties, Sérusier had been guided by Gauguin as he painted the small canvas *Landscape at the Bois d'Amour at Pont-Aven (The Talisman)* (Plate 19). This famous painting was executed according to the most typically synthetic precepts of Gauguin's theories. Among Sérusier's colleagues in Paris were Maurice Denis, Paul Ranson, Henri-Gabriel Ibels, Ker-Xavier Roussel, Pierre Bonnard, and Edouard Vuillard. Aristide Maillol, who later dedicated himself to sculpture and became the most important exponent of Symbolism in the plastic arts, was also in contact with this group.

What is interesting about these young people is that they did not limit themselves merely to working together and to discussing art. Rather, they set out to form a true community of their own, in which Symbolist precepts permeated the way of life, even to the way they dressed. They took up and adapted to their needs a ritual inspired by oriental mysticism. They called themselves Nabis, from a Hebrew word meaning "prophet." Each member had a specific role. Denis was "the Nabi of beautiful icons," Bonnard the "very Japanese Nabi" because of his love of Japanese prints, and so on. The place where they met, the Atelier Ranson, was called The Temple. Ceremonial garments and elaborate rituals completed this attempt to escape the banality of everyday life. By setting themselves apart in this ritualistic community, the Nabis created a stimulating atmosphere for productive work.

These young artists were very much concerned with the quality of life around them, and rather than escape, their purpose was actively to reform customs, fashion, and politics. They tried to widen their art to encompass all aspects of life in a vast Symbolist tide. Unlike Gauguin and van Gogh, who were eternal pilgrims seeking a vision that lay always beyond them, the Nabis almost never left Paris except for pleasure trips or to study.

This second Symbolist generation, who had come on the scene after the great breakthroughs had been made, tried to avoid the anguished struggles and polemics that had characterized the pioneers. The aim of the Nabis was to continue the innovations of Symbolism, but in an atmosphere of relaxed and serene experimentation, and to avoid the dissensions and drama that had marked the careers of the earlier artists. This was a generation capable of distinguishing between reality and fiction and of sustaining its visions and high ideals even when living in the heart of the French capital.

The kind of deep and discriminating intelligence typical of the Nabis made Sérusier and Denis excellent theorists as well as artists. They were in complete agreement with the ideas of Aurier as stated in his Symbolist doctrine. Sérusier compiled an *ABC of Painting* in which the virtue of certain "primary" values was stressed. He wrote of distributing values harmoniously, through a conscious, rhythmic balance of elements in the painting. This complex formalism was not intended to be an end in itself, but was rather to be a guide in the illumination of the truths of this world and of the universe.

Maurice Denis composed an aphorism while he was still young that later became famous: "Remember that before a painting becomes a battle charger, a nude woman, or any other representation, it is essentially a plain surface covered by colors that are united by a certain order." This single sentence is a statement of all the principles of the Symbolist concept of synthesis. If the last phrase of Denis's sentence seems to prophesy art trends of the twentieth century, it would be a mistake to assume that he was anticipating the development of abstract art. According to Denis, the "order" of colors and shapes traced on a two-dimensional surface is not meant to describe the ultimate and exclusive limits of artistic creativity; rather, it implies the necessity of some magical influence or obscure celestial power. For this reason Denis's rhetoric remains limited to the Symbolist sphere and cannot be applied beyond it.

That Denis was completely responsive to the precepts of Symbolism can be confirmed by examining his paintings. From the most daring ones done early in the 1890s through those of the twentieth century, his work maintained a heavily plastic technique reminiscent of Bernard's. In some of Denis's best works, such as *April* (Plate 42) and *The Muses* (Plate 41), we can see that he keeps.that supreme harmony of surfaces dictated by his theories even when the subject matter (young girls, trees, and spring vegetation) almost demands a different approach. The rich, flexible line achieved through extravagant strokes constitutes the stylistic hallmark of the entire Symbolist movement. In Denis's paintings, this line is used to represent such diverse concepts as feminine grace and liturgical elements of the Catholic religion.

The paintings of Sérusier appear less original and experimental, especially the early ones made when he was under Gauguin's influence. The work he did in Brittany closely follows the example of his teacher, differing only in that it is more subtle and elegant—more akin to Bernard's "neo-Gothic" style.

Paul Ranson was much more daring. Ranson, who was aggressively nonreligious, ignored the mystical and religious themes used by his fellow Nabis. Instead, his paintings were based on "modern life." They were not in the Naturalist tradition in any sense, but expressed everyday forms in linear patterns that have been called the most exciting of the entire Symbolist period. Georges Lacombe was no less daring. A good example of his work is the extraordinary *Gray Sea* (Plate 32). In this painting a primitive, almost childlike representation is joined with a sophisticated study of most unusual arrangement, so much so that the painting becomes an enigma that is hard to read.

Roussel, Vuillard, and Bonnard have one characteristic in common: From the beginning all three followed the teachings of their group and therefore abided by the canons of synthesis and the use of flat color. Their intense sensuality soon led them, however, to a technique characterized by rich pigmentation laid down by broken brushstrokes, rapidly and spontaneously executed. Roussel preferred to concentrate on nature and depicted pastoral scenes filled with trees and mythological apparitions. The "twins" Vuillard and Bonnard, on the other hand, took up *la peinture de la vie moderne,* that is, the painting of modern life. The specialized particularly in interiors, handling them with great audacity by using sudden disruptions and unusual design and perspective. This experiment was true to Symbolist interests.

A unique combination of the preference for interiors and the Symbolist linear pattern was achieved by the least involved of the Nabis, Félix Vallotton. This is seen especially in his paintings of 1890 in which a detailed, realistic treatment of objects and figures is often accompanied by a vigorous synthetic spirit, beautifully sinuous contours, and successful stylization.

The Posters of Toulouse-Lautrec

One of the best known artists of the time, Henri de Toulouse-Lautrec, remained outside the movement despite his association with the Symbolist group that met at the studio of Cormon. His drive to become an artist was so great that he broke away from the traditions of his aristocratic family, to live a bohemian life in Paris. It is important to note that the abbreviated and modeled style developed by Toulouse-Lautrec had a goal quite different from that of the Symbolists, as can be seen in his 1886 painting *Cirque Fernando: The Equestrienne* (Plate 57). Toulouse-Lautrec was never moved by the desire for flight or by a vague longing for mysterious principles beyond the certainty of the here and now. He remained totally fascinated by the life around him and eager to portray all its aspects. We may be certain that Lautrec was never intellectually a Symbolist, even though he used many of the same techniques. This can best be illustrated by looking at poster-making, which was of such interest at that time. Posters lend themselves particularly well to the demands of synthesis. Because of the materialistic nature of posters, we also find the artists working in this field tending toward a worldly rather than a religious viewpoint.

The first poster to bring the new way of synthesis to public notice was *France-Champagne,* designed in 1891 by the Nabi painter Pierre Bonnard. The style he used had, of course, been employed very successfully before, but its recognition was limited to intellectual circles. Lautrec was excited by the possibilities in Bonnard's poster and inspired to create the vivid scenes that began with his famous posters for the Folies-Bergere. The series continued with commissions from the Jardin de Paris, Aristide Bruant, book publishers, and theaters. His compositions were based on the daring "Chinese shadows," which was oblique and distorted. But the linear distortions were attuned to the features of the people or the pictorial aspects of the objects he represented. The nobleman turned artist never made the mistake of trying to give a feeling of hidden natural forces, as did Maurice Denis in his posters.

Félix Vallotton occupied a special position in this minor feud between the worldly artists and the mystics, or to define the viewpoints differently, the "painters of modern life" and the Symbolists. Although he never designed posters, Vallotton did make a series of graphic illustrations and woodcuts in a somewhat popular vein to show the disenchanted, petty spirit of "modern life." However, in his oil paintings and especially in his woodcuts, we find great skill in the use of serpentine lines, although any mystical feeling has been inhibited. This can be contrasted with the work of Denis, who felt at ease with the soft, sensuous lines demanded by the Symbolist spirit.

Conclusion

Looking back at our brief study of the Symbolist movement, we can see that it was an evolution in technique that began with the Impressionists, who were often the teachers of the artists who were to be called Symbolists. In their experiments with light and color, the Impressionists had shown that meaning is within the province of technique as well as of subject matter. The painters of the Symbolist movement continued to experiment with technique, but in some ways they seemed to have taken a step backward. In their concern with definition of form and with flat color in carefully delineated areas, they seemed to have much in common with the Naturalists. Closer examination shows that the Symbolists' emphasis on form and outline was only for the sake of identifying the subject and giving it a physical attribute so that the painter could then search beyond the physical reality for the hidden essence. It was the search for the "something beyond," the deeper spiritual reality, that led Seurat to develop Divisionism, Gauguin to experiment with large, flat areas of color, and van Gogh to develop and emphasize the curving, sinuous brushstroke. Thus they attempted to synthesize, or join in one painting, the Natural and the underlying, deeper truth of the Ideal. How well they succeeded is evident when we look at the promenaders of Seurat, the Tahitian women of Gauguin, or the fields of van Gogh. In all these paintings we can recognize the objects represented for what they are, but simultaneously we know that there is more. The very use of color and curving lines suggests that beyond the physical attributes of *this* promenader, *this* woman of the South Seas, and *this* olive tree lies a reality of spirit and essence that links everything in an arcane meaning.

All this becomes clear if we contrast the courageously experimental avant-garde painters we have discussed with some minor artists who were their contemporaries. In this latter group it is possible to see a gap between the themes dealt with and the artists' ability to handle them technically. The themes were conventionally lofty: nobility of character, literary images, old myths, and fantasy. The means of expressing the themes were, however, trite and popular. We can see this in the posters of the Czech artist Alphonse Mucha and in the stained glass and tapestries of Eugène Grasset. Both of these men aped the flexible curves of the Symbolists but smothered them in an abundance of decoration. The relative failure of these artists underlines the problems that the Symbolists sought to solve: Their aim was to unite the spiritual and metaphysical content of the Idealists with the cogent reality of the Naturalists.

PLATES

The Generation of the Idealists

PLATE 2 GUSTAVE MOREAU *Orpheus at the Tomb of Eurydice,* 1897–98 (174 x 128 cm) Paris, Musée Gustave Moreau

PLATE 3 GUSTAVE MOREAU *Narcissus, c.* 1895 (53 x 61 cm) Paris, Musée Gustave Moreau

PLATE 4 PIERRE PUVIS DE CHAVANNES *The Poor Fisherman*, 1881 (152 x 190 cm) Paris, Musée du Louvre

The Beginning of Symbolism in Painting

PLATE 5 EUGÈNE CARRIÈRE *Grief, c.* 1900 (41 x 33 cm) Otterlo, The Netherlands, Rijksmuseum Kröller-Müller

PLATE 6 ODILON REDON *Phantasmagoria* (22 x 27 cm) Bordeaux, Musée des Beaux-Arts

PLATE 7   ODILON REDON *Pandora, c.* 1910 (143.5 x 62.2 cm)
New York, Metropolitan Museum of Art (Bequest of
Alexander M. Bing)

PLATE 8 ODILON REDON *Portrait of Violette Heymann,* 1909–10 (72 x 92.5 cm) Cleveland, Ohio, Cleveland Museum of Art, Hinman B. Hurlbut Collection

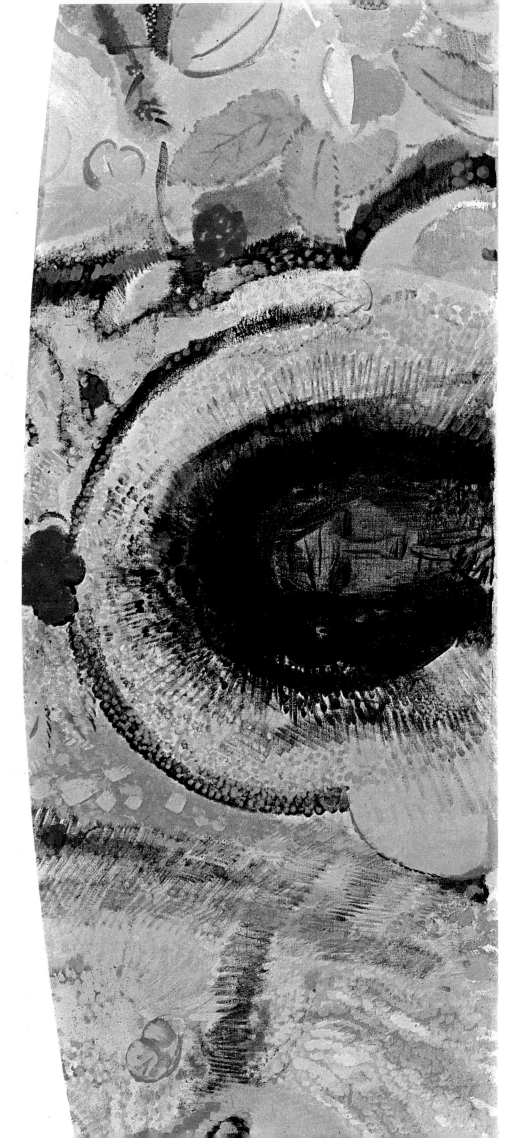

PLATE 9   ODILON REDON *Silence*, 1910–11 (46 x 106 cm) (Detail from *La Nuit*, 200 x 650 cm) Fontfroide, France, Gustave Fayet, Bibliothèque de l'Abbaye de Fontfroide

PLATE 10   ODILON REDON *Roger and Angelica*, 1909–10 (30 x 29 cm) Otterlo, The Netherlands, Rijksmuseum Kröller-Müller

PLATE 11   ODILON REDON *Vase of Flowers,* 1914 (73 x 53.7 cm) New York, Museum of Modern Art (Gift of
William S. Paley)

Symbolistic Elements in the Art of Seurat

PLATE 12   GEORGES SEURAT *The Stone Breaker, c.* 1882 (19.5 x 28.5 cm) Upperville, Virginia, Mr. and Mrs. Paul Mellon Collection

PLATE 13   GEORGES SEURAT *La Parade*, 1887–88 (99.2 x 149.9 cm) New York, Metropolitan Museum of Art (Bequest of Stephen C. Clark, 1960)

31

PLATE 14   GEORGES SEURAT *The Circus*, 1890–91 (179.5 x 148 cm) Paris, Musée du Louvre

PLATE 15   Georges Seurat *Le Chahut*, 1889–90 (169 x 139 cm) Otterlo, The Netherlands, Rijksmuseum Kröller-Müller

Gauguin, Bernard and the School of Pont-Aven

PLATE 16   PAUL GAUGUIN *Seashore at Martinique*, 1887 (54.5 x 89.5 cm) Copenhagen, Ny Carlsberg Glyptotek

PLATE 17   PAUL GAUGUIN *Cows at the Watering Place*, 1885 (80 x 65 cm) Milan, Galleria d'Arte Moderna, Grassi Collection

PLATE 18   PAUL GAUGUIN *The Yellow Christ*, 1889 (92 x 73 cm) Buffalo, Albright-Knox Art Gallery

PLATE 19   PAUL SÉRUSIER *Landscape at the Bois d'Amour at Pont-Aven (The Talisman)*, 1888 (27 x 22 cm) Paris, Family of Maurice Denis

PLATE 20   PAUL GAUGUIN *La Belle Angèle (Mme. Angèle Satre)*, 1889 (92 x 73 cm) Paris, Musée du Louvre

PLATE 21   EMILE BERNARD *Breton Women under Umbrellas,* 1892 (81 x 100 cm) Paris, Musée National d'Art Moderne

PLATE 22   PAUL GAUGUIN *The Vision after the Sermon (Jacob Wrestling with the Angel)*, 1888 (73 x 92 cm) Edinburgh, National Gallery of Scotland

PLATE 23   PAUL GAUGUIN *Where do we come from? What are we? Where are we going?*, 1897 (141 × 376 cm) Boston, Museum of Fine Arts

PLATE 24   EMILE BERNARD *Medieval Scene*, 1892 (63 x 93 cm) Munich, Galleria del Levante

PLATE 25   EMILE BERNARD *Harvest by the Sea*, 1891 (73 x 92 cm) Paris, M. Clément Altarriba Collection

Vincent van Gogh

PLATE 27   VINCENT VAN GOGH *Sunflowers*, 1888 (92.5 x 73 cm) Amsterdam, Vincent van Gogh Foundation (On loan to
the Stedelijk Museum, Amsterdam)

PLATE 28   VINCENT VAN GOGH *Wheatfield with Crows,* 1890 (51 x 103.5 cm) Amsterdam, Vincent van Gogh Foundation
(On loan to the Stedelijk Museum, Amsterdam)

PLATE 29   VINCENT VAN GOGH *Road with Cypress and Star,* 1890 (92 x 73 cm) Otterlo, The Netherlands, Rijksmuseum Kröller-Müller

PLATE 30   GEORGES LACOMBE *The Black Rams, c.* 1892 (58 x 77 cm) Munich, Galleria del Levante

PLATE 31   PAUL SÉRUSIER *Notre-Dame des Portes* (91 x 72 cm) Quimper, Musée des Beaux-Arts

PLATE 32   GEORGES LACOMBE *Gray Sea, c.* 1890 (82 x 61 cm) Munich, Galleria del Levante

PLATE 33   PAUL SÉRUSIER *Meditation, c.* 1890 (71 x 58 cm) Paris, Mlle. Henriette Boutaric Collection

PLATE 34   PAUL RANSON *Nudes with Lion, c.* 1890 (72 x 90 cm) Rome, Galleria del Levante

PLATE 35   PIERRE BONNARD *Portrait of Andrée Bonnard,* 1890
(188 x 80 cm) Paris, Terrasse Collection

54

PLATE 37   PAUL RANSON *Bather, c.* 1890 (61 x 50 cm) Rome, Galleria del Levante

PLATE 36   PAUL RANSON *Girl with Flowers, c.* 1890 (150 x 70 cm) Rome, Galleria del Levante

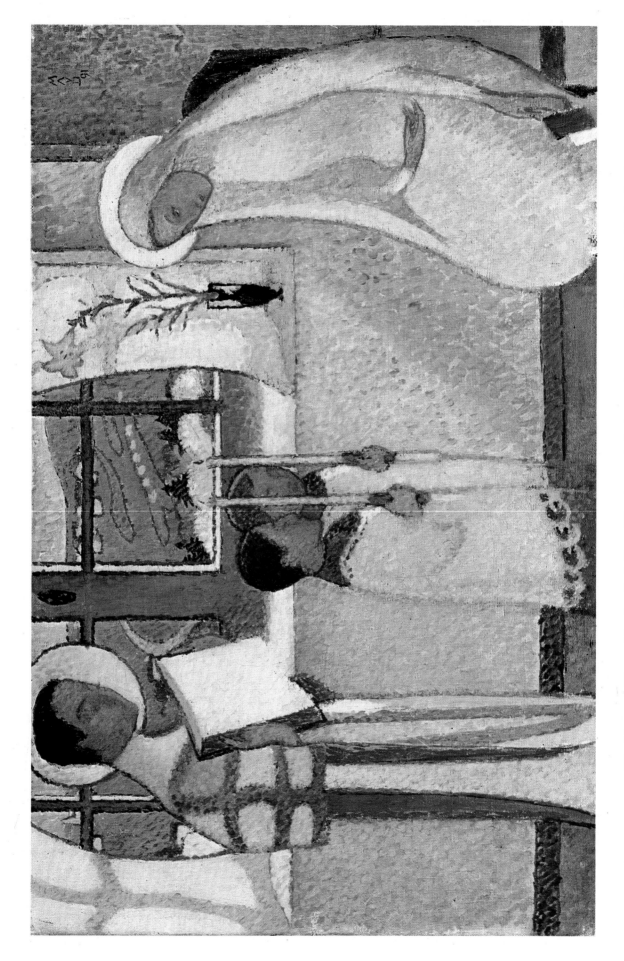

PLATE 38   MAURICE DENIS *Mystère Catholique (The Annunciation)*, 1891 (27 x 41 cm) Otterlo, The Netherlands, Rijksmuseum Kröller-Müller

PLATE 39   KER-XAVIER ROUSSEL *Milking the Goat*, 1891 (25 x 39 cm) Paris, Salomon Collection

PLATE 40   PIERRE BONNARD *The Croquet Game,* 1892 (130 x 162 cm) Paris, Private Collection

PLATE 41   MAURICE DENIS *The Muses*, 1893 (168 x 135 cm) Paris, Musée National d'Art Moderne

PLATE 42   MAURICE DENIS *April*, 1892 (37.5 x 61 cm) Otterlo, The Netherlands, Rijksmuseum Kröller-Müller

60

PLATE 43 Félix Vallotton *The Bath on a Summer Afternoon,* 1892 (93 x 131 cm) Zurich, Kunsthaus

PLATE 44 GEORGES LACOMBE *Harvesting Buckwheat in Brittany*, 1895 (48 x 63 cm) Paris, Edouard Monod-Herzen Collection

PLATE 45   ARISTIDE MAILLOL *The Music*, 1895 (45 × 55 cm) Munich, Galleria del Levante

PLATE 46   FÉLIX VALLOTTON *Moonlight,* 1895 (27 x 41 cm) Milan, Dr. V. Olcese Collection

PLATE 47   KER-XAVIER ROUSSEL *The Window* (121 x 92 cm) Zurich, Walter Feilchenfeldt Collection

PLATE 48   EDOUARD VUILLARD *Decoration for the House of Dr. Vaquez,* 1896 (213 x 154 cm) Paris, Musée du Petit-Palais

PLATE 49-50   EDOUARD VUILLARD *Decoration for the House of Dr. Vaquez,* 1896 (212 x 77 cm) Paris, Musée du Petit-Palais

PLATE 51   FÉLIX VALLOTTON *Women with Cats,* 1898 (50 x 69 cm) Lausanne, Claude Vallotton Collection

PLATE 52   PAUL RANSON *Woman in Red, c.* 1893 (150 x 100 cm) Paris, Ranson Collection

PLATE 53   PAUL SÉRUSIER *Breton in Cornfield, c.* 1895 (50 x 61 cm) Munich, Galleria del Levante

PLATE 54   MAURICE DENIS *Vacation Homework,* 1934 (37 x 35 cm) Albi, France, Musée Toulouse-Lautrec

Symbolism and Art Nouveau

PLATE 55   LOUIS ANQUETIN *Pont Neuf in Paris,* 1889 (118 x 125 cm) Munich, Galleria del Levante

PLATE 56   HENRI DE TOULOUSE-LAUTREC *Loïe Fuller at the Folies Bergère*, 1893 (63 x 45 cm) Albi, France, Musée Toulouse-Lautrec

PLATE 57 HENRI DE TOULOUSE-LAUTREC *Cirque Fernando: The Equestrienne*, 1888 (98.5 x 161.5 cm) Chicago, Art Institute of Chicago, Joseph Winterbotham Collection

PLATE 58   HENRI DE TOULOUSE-LAUTREC *Jane Avril, Jardin de Paris*, 1892 (60.5 x 41.5 cm) Albi, France, Musée Toulouse-Lautrec

PLATE 59   ALPHONSE MUCHA *Médée* (Sarah Bernhardt as Medea),
            1898 (208 x 77 cm) Paris, Bibliothèque du Musée des
            Arts Décoratifs

PLATE 60   EUGENE GRASSET *Spring* (Stained-glass window by Félix Gaudin workshop), 1884 (294 x 132 cm)
Paris, Musée des Arts Décoratifs

IMP. F. CHAMPENOIS. 66.Boul.^d St Michel. PARIS

PLATE 61   ALPHONSE MUCHA *Job,* 1898 (150 x 100 cm) Paris, Bibliothèque du Musée des Arts Décoratifs

THE ARTISTS

LOUIS ANQUETIN

Born in Etrépagny in 1861. He enrolled at the studio of Cormon in Paris, where he became friendly with Bernard and Toulouse-Lautrec, and along with them became a member of the "Groupe Petit Boulevard" between 1886 and 1887. In 1888

SÉRUSIER *Portrait of Emile Bernard in Florence*, 1893 (73 x 60 cm) Paris, Mlle. Henriette Boutaric Collection

he showed his paintings at an exhibition in Brussels presented by a group of artists known as "Les XX." Soon after, he became associated with the artists who formed the Pont-Aven and Nabi groups. He died in Paris in 1932.

EMILE BERNARD

Born in Lille in 1868. When he was sixteen he joined the studio of Cormon in Paris, where he became friendly with Toulouse-Lautrec. He was expelled from the studio because of his restless, intolerant character. His stay at Pont-Aven with Paul Gauguin in 1888 was decisive for him. He developed Cloisonnisme there with his friend Anquetin. He founded and directed a magazine called *La Rénovation Esthétique* and gave several lectures. An enthusiastic admirer of van Gogh, Redon, and Cézanne, he helped make their artistic merits known.

In 1893 Bernard went to Italy and Egypt. He was

ANQUETIN *Portrait of Toulouse-Lautrec*, 1889 (61 x 39 cm) Albi, France, Musée Toulouse-Lautrec

BERNARD *Portrait of Water on the Beach*, 1893 (85 x 45 cm) Paris, Michel-Ange Bernard-Fort Collection

81

fascinated by the works of the Venetian masters and tried to develop a style similar to theirs, but as years went by his work became progressively more complex. He died in Paris in 1941.

PIERRE BONNARD

Born at Fontenay-aux-Roses in the outskirts of Paris on October 3, 1867, he spent his childhood there. He was an excellent high-school student and in 1887 enrolled in the Law School of the University of Paris, but his interests were poetry, philosophy, and painting, and he did not prove to be a good law student. He studied at the Ecole des Beaux-Arts and the School of Interior Design, and then joined the Academy Julian, where he met Vuillard, Roussel, Denis, Sérusier, Ranson, and Ibels. All these artists later formed the group of the Nabis. After a brief period of military service he opened a studio in Paris with Vuillard and Denis.

BONNARD *The Laundry Girl,* 1896 (30 x 19 cm)

In 1891 he designed his first poster (for a champagne producer) and made some lithographs for *La Revue Blanche,* a magazine founded by the Natanson brothers, to which he was an active contributor. In 1892 and 1893 he exhibited at the Independent Show, and in 1896 he had a one-man show at the Durand-Ruel Gallery. He also did scene-painting in collaboration with Sérusier. He had achieved international fame by 1897 and exhibited in Sweden and Norway. He illustrated many literary works during the first years of this century, among which were Verlaine's *Parallèlement,* Renard's *Histoires Naturelles,* and Mirbeau's *La 628-E8.* In 1903 he took part in the artistic movement of the "Secession" of Vienna (an Art Nouveau style) and, in 1908, the one in Munich.

His later years were marked by a series of exhibits and trips, including Holland and England in 1913, and the United States in 1926. He retired to Le Cannet, near Cannes, in 1925 and there his wife, Marthe, who had inspired so many of his paintings, died in 1942. Five years later, on January 23, 1947, he died in the same place.

CARRIÈRE *Puvis de Chavannes,* 1897 (54.6 x 39.5 cm)

EUGÈNE CARRIÈRE

Born in Gournay (Seine-et-Marne) in 1848 and spent his childhood in Strasbourg. In 1870 he enrolled at the Académie des Beaux-Arts in Paris, where he studied under Cabanel from 1872 to 1876. His painting *Mother and Child,* a subject he often chose, was accepted by the Salon of 1879. He became friendly with Gauguin about 1890 and painted his portrait, in exchange for which he

DENIS *Apparition, Poem by Stéphanie Mallarmé, Music by André Rossignol*

received a Gauguin self-portrait. He was the author of two essays, *L'enseignement et l'éducation de l'art par la vie,* and *L'homme visionnaire de la réalité,* published respectively in 1900 and 1903. He died in Paris in 1906.

MAURICE DENIS

Born in Granville on November 25, 1870. His home both in childhood and for the rest of his life was in Saint-Germain-en-Laye, near Paris. After having attended high school in Paris, he joined the group of young artists called the Nabis, which was formed in 1888.

In 1891 he exhibited paintings at the first show of Le Barc de Bouteville Gallery, along with other Nabis. He became one of the most convinced defenders of Symbolist art (*Théories, Nouvelles Théories*). He travelled extensively in Belgium, Germany, Spain, Switzerland, Algeria, the United States, Canada, Greece, and Palestine. But it was by Italy that he was most profoundly influenced — his love for all the most sublime aspects of nature and art was especially nourished in Rome, Siena, Florence, and Assisi. He died at Saint-Germain-en-Laye on November 3, 1943.

PAUL GAUGUIN

Born in Paris on June 7, 1848, he spent four years of his childhood in Lima, Peru, with his family. He returned to Orléans, France, and completed his

studies, and in 1865 went to sea as a crewman on a freight ship. After this he did his military service in the navy; he joined the French brokerage firm of Bertin and became a successful businessman. In 1873 he married a Danish girl, Mette-Sophie Gad. In his free time, he painted in the company of his colleague Emile Schuffenecker. In 1876 the Salon accepted one of his paintings, and from 1880 on he took part in all the Impressionist exhibits. He then found himself in the balance between the world of finance and the world of art. He chose painting and, in 1883, without even telling his wife of his plans, he left his job, feverishly determined to dedicate himself to his art, and abandoned his family in Copenhagen. After a futile attempt to reconcile his two worlds, he prepared himself to overcome all obstacles, including poverty, illness, and the misunderstanding of those who laughed at his work.

After staying in Rouen and Copenhagen, Gauguin returned to France in June, 1885, and started frequent trips between Paris and Brittany. He became friendly with a young artist named

GAUGUIN *Self-Portrait: "Les Miserables,"* 1888 (45 x 55 cm) Amsterdam, Vincent van Gogh Foundation, Theo van Gogh Collection

Charles Laval and sailed with him to Panama and then to Martinique, but after Gauguin fell ill, they returned to Paris penniless. His good friend Schuffenecker gave him board in Paris, where he became a friend of the van Gogh brothers, who were great admirers of his work. In Paris he often frequented the Symbolist meetings at the Café Voltaire, forming friendships with Mallarmé, Aurier, Morice, Redon, Carrière, the Nabis painters, and Mirbeau.

In 1891 he decided to leave France for the tropics. His first trip to Tahiti was neither long nor happy, but he still became addicted to its climate, its natural surroundings, and its freedom. He returned to Paris in August, 1893, and remained until February, 1895. But in Paris he had nothing but disappointment: His exhibit at the Durand-Ruel Gallery was not successful, his auction sale was disastrous, his visit to his wife in Copenhagen led nowhere, he quickly spent a small inheritance, and his Javanese mistress, Anna, ransacked his studio and ran off.

After Gauguin left for Tahiti at the beginning of 1895, he never returned to France. Suffering from loneliness, he attempted to commit suicide in 1898. Right afterward, he clashed with the island government and in 1901 left Tahiti to take refuge on the island of Dominica in the Marquesas. There he became seriously ill and even considered returning to France. The Marquesas government sensed the danger that this white man held for them when he defended the natives and in March, 1903, condemned him to three months in prison. For Gauguin this was the end. Overcome by worries, consumed by illness, and consoled only by the words of Vernier, a Protestant minister, Gauguin died on May 8, 1903.

EUGÈNE GRASSET

Born in Lausanne in 1841. He became an architect

GRASSET *Salon of the 100-Exhibit of E. Grasset, 1894*

in his native city, and after a stay in Egypt in 1869, he settled in Paris, where he became friendly with an architect named Viollet-le-Duc. He was a painter and illustrator and took an interest in all forms of art. His art was functional and decorative, and he wrote several essays that made him one of the greatest defenders of Art Nouveau. He died in Lausanne in 1917.

GEORGES LACOMBE

Born in Versailles of a wealthy family in 1868. At eighteen he already had a beautiful studio, which the Nabis called *ergastère* and which Sérusier decorated in 1893. He worked with Alfred Roll for a while, joined the Academy Julian, and established contact with the Nabis painters. He died in Alençon in 1916. He is remembered more for his sculpture than for his paintings.

ARISTIDE MAILLOL

Born in Banyuls-sur-Mer in 1861. In 1885 he enrolled in the Beaux-Arts Academy in Paris and had Gérôme, Cabanel, and Laurens for his teachers. Painting was the art form that interested him, and he profoundly admired Gauguin and Cézanne. He came in contact with the Nabis group, which kept him as an adviser.

He designed some sketches for tapestries at Banyuls, specifying even their texture. But the wool dyes gave him an eye disease, which forced him to stop this line of work. Once cured, he turned to sculpture. His forceful feminine nudes became famous. He died in his late eighties in 1914, at Banyuls.

GUSTAVE MOREAU

Born in Paris in 1826. His trip to Italy in 1857 was decisive in his career, for there he discovered the fifteenth-century masters. In 1880 he began teaching at the Ecole des Beaux-Arts, where Rouault, Matisse, Albert Marquet, Jan Puy, and Evenepoel were among his students. He respected their personalities and never imposed his views on them. His art is filled with mystical literary motifs, early manifestations of Symbolism. He died in Paris in 1898.

ALPHONSE MUCHA

Born in Ivanice (Czechoslovakia) in 1860 and studied at the Beaux-Arts Academy of Prague. He then went on to the Munich Academy and in 1890 moved to Paris. He achieved success as a poster designer. Among his works were posters of Sarah Bernhardt. He died in Prague in 1939.

PIERRE PUVIS DE CHAVANNES

Born in Lyon in 1824 into a family of long-established lawyers. He died in Paris in 1898. His art was influenced by the works of Henri Scheffer, Thomas Couture, and Eugène Delacroix and by a visit to Italy. Toward the end of the nineteenth century, when painting on canvas on an easel seemed to be the only means of expression for an artist, he turned to murals and passionately defended their pictorial technique. It was only toward the end of his life that his art began to be appreciated and he was given official awards.

PAUL RANSON

Born in Limoges in 1864 into a well-to-do family. Encouraged by his relatives, he began his artistic career early in life. After studying at the Academy of Decorative Arts at Limoges, he enrolled in the one in Paris, but he soon left it for the Academy Julian. Here he became part of the Nabis group, which began meeting every Saturday at Ranson's studio. In 1891 he took part in the first exhibit of the group at Le Barc de Boutteville Gallery; he also participated in all subsequent exhibits. He designed several tapestries under Maillol's influence.

In 1908 he founded the Paul Ranson Academy with his wife who, after the painter's death (on February 20, 1909), became its director. Some of the Nabis painters were teachers at the Ranson Academy.

ODILON REDON

Born in Bordeaux in April, 1840. He spent his childhood in Peyrelebade, in the neighboring countryside, looked after by a nurse and then by an old uncle. There he lived in natural surround-

ings that were free and still half-wild, removed from his parents (who lived in Bordeaux) and from friends of his own age. Owing to his delicate health, he did not start school until he was eleven.

Between the ages of fifteen and eighteen he studied design with the artist Stanislas Gorin. His friendships with the botanical scientist Armand Clavaud, and with Rodolphe Bresdin, the engraver, influenced him greatly as a young man. He especially admired Leonardo da Vinci and Rembrandt. Among the modern painters, he was interested in Delacroix's use of color and he admired the magic, unreal atmosphere in Moreau's paintings. He was profoundly dissatisfied with

REDON *Vision* (Plate VIII from *Dans le Rêve*), 1879 (27.4 x 19.8 cm)

Gérôme's academic teachings, and in reaction to them started doing charcoal drawings. Later, encouraged by Fantin-Latour, he took many of the themes he had developed in his charcoals and made engravings. Engraving and lithography were his principal occupations until 1890. The first collection of his lithographs, *Dans le Rêve*, appeared in 1879. Before 1884 (the year in which he, Seurat, and Signac founded the Society of Independent Artists), he had published *Edgar A. Poe* and *Les Origines.* Later on he illustrated famous texts, such as Flaubert's *La Tentation de Saint Antoine* and Baudelaire's *Les Fleurs du Mal* (1890). At that time, Redon's work was still misunderstood

MOREAU *Jupiter and Semele* (143 x 110 cm)

85

by most critics and the general public. Among the few who appreciated him were certain collectors, Bonger, Frizeau, Fayet, and the Symbolist writers Joris-Karl Huysmans and Mallarmé, who became his close friends.

About 1890 he finally turned to oil painting and pastels. His work began to become popular and he received commissions to paint portraits and decorative works for private residences. Among them was the decoration for the Abbey of Font-froide, owned by Gustave Fayet, which Redon did between 1910 and 1911 and which is considered one of his masterpieces. He spent a quiet old age in the company of family and friends and always managed to preserve a young and optimistic outlook. He died in Paris on July 6, 1916.

KER-XAVIER ROUSSEL

Born in Chêne, near Lorry-les-Metz, on December 10, 1867. He studied at the Condorcet School, where he became friends with Vuillard, with whom he later attended Diogène Maillard's studio. Some time later, at the Academy Julian, he joined the Nabis group and exhibited his works at their 1891 show. In 1893 he married Marie Vuillard, his close friend's sister.

On a bicycle trip that he took with Denis from Marseille to Menton, he visited Cézanne and remained very impressed by him. His painting was influenced by the hot Mediterranean regions. He died at Etang-la-Ville on June 6, 1944.

PAUL SÉRUSIER

Born in Paris in 1863. As a student, he was more interested in philosophy and Oriental languages than in art. At twenty-three he enrolled at the Academy Julian. His art was academic until, in 1888, he met Gauguin on a trip to Brittany and under his guidance painted the *Landscape at the Bois d'Amour*. This painting, which he showed his friends at the Academy Julian (Denis, Ibels, Bonnard, Ranson, Vuillard, and Roussel), became a source of inspiration, the "talisman" that gave life to the Nabis group. The following year, Sérusier returned to Brittany to paint with Gauguin. In 1891 he became friendly with Jan Verkade, a Dutch painter who joined the Nabis group, and that same year he took part in the first Nabis exhibit at Le Barc de Boutteville Gallery. He formed part of the Théâtre de L'Oeuvre founded by Lugné-Poë and made several trips to Italy with Denis (1895, 1899, and 1904). In 1908 he began teaching at the Ranson Academy. In 1914, he retired to Brittany. Seven years later, the book in which he expressed his theories, *L'ABC de la Peinture,* was published. He died in Morlaix in 1927.

GEORGES SEURAT

Born in Paris in December, 1859. In 1878, he enrolled at the Beaux-Arts Academy. He was influenced by Ingres, Delacroix, and Puvis de

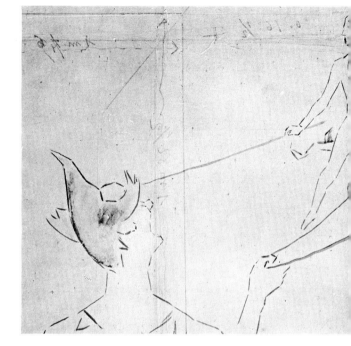

SEURAT *Study for "The Circus,"* 1890 (30 x 23.5 cm) Paris, Cabinet des Dessins, Musée du Louvre

Chavannes, and remained deeply impressed by the Fourth Impressionist Exhibit. He became interested in the scientific treatises of Chevreul and other scientists and tried to apply their theories to painting, for he was convinced that color had to be used according to precise, constant laws. From 1881 to 1883 he dedicated himself to working in black and white.

Bathing at Asnières, his first major work, was rejected by the Salon in 1884, and he then exhibited it at the show of the Group of Independent Artists. He met Paul Signac at one of the meetings on the formation of the Society of Independent Artists, and their encounter proved fruitful for their artistic development. In collaboration with Signac, Seurat perfected the system of his artistic technique, the result of which was *A Sunday Afternoon on the Island of La Grande-Jatte*. In 1886 Camille Pissarro, who, with his son Lucien, had recently adhered to Seurat's ideas, succeeded in having him and Signac admitted to the Eighth Impressionist Show. There, with other works, Seurat exhibited his *Grande-Jatte*, which was misunderstood by the general public and laughed at by the critics. Among the few who appreciated his works were van Gogh, Verhaeren, the Belgian Symbolist poet, and, above all, the critic Félix Fénéon, who from then on became the speaker for the movement, which he named Neo-Impressionism. Seurat exhibited his *Grande-Jatte* at the Independent show that same year and at the show of *Les XX* in Brussels the following year.

Meanwhile, an ever-growing number of artists began to join Seurat and his Divisionist theories. After Signac and the two Pissarros came Albert Dubois-Pillet, Charles Angrand, Henri-Edmond Cross, Maximilien Luce, Léo Gausson, Hippolyte Petitjean, and the Belgian artists Willy Finch, Théo van Rysselberghe and Georges Lemmen. Around 1890 their first disagreement arose and Camille Pissarro and others abandoned the Divisionist movement.

Up to 1886 Seurat was influenced by Charles Henry's theories on the symbolic value of lines and colors. This influence is easily recognizable in *La Parade* (1887–1888), *Le Chahut* (1889–1890) and *The Circus* (1890–1891). On March 29, 1891, Seurat died at thirty-one years of age after only two days of illness. His son was stricken by the same disease and died two weeks later.

SEURAT *Study for "La Grande-Jatte,"* c. 1884

HENRI DE TOULOUSE-LAUTREC

Born in Albi on November 24, 1864 into an aristocratic family. In 1873 he moved with his family to Paris, where he attended the Fontanes school.

TOULOUSE-LAUTREC
Advertisement for a Bicycle

Later he studied privately because of health reasons. His sketches of horses and caricatures of his teachers showed his drawing abilities early in his life. But perhaps he would never have taken painting seriously had he not suffered two dangerous falls (1878 and 1879) which prevented his legs from growing any further. But he reacted with great strength of will to his misfortunes and through his drawings was able to conquer the sadness and boredom of the long hours of immobility. René Princeteau, a deaf and dumb artist friend of his father, finally encouraged him to dedicate himself entirely to painting. In the fall of 1882, he entered Bonnat's studio and remained there until the following spring. He spent the summer at Albi, painting portraits that showed a remarkable technical development. When he returned to Paris he began to attend Cormon's studio, where he remained until 1886 and made friends with many of his fellow students, including van Gogh.

In 1884 he rented an apartment in Montmartre, where he remained until 1897. It was in this bohemian neighborhood that Lautrec discovered his world—the type of thoughtless, bitter, frenetic life he led was a constant source of inspiration. In 1893, he exhibited his works inspired by Montmartre at the Goupil Gallery. He had moderate success and gained the approval of the famous Degas. The theater also attracted him a great deal, and he designed programs and posters for various shows and made paintings and lithographs of several famous actors and actresses. His friend Tristan Bernard introduced him to the world of sport, where he found new interests.

In 1895 he went to London and there met Whistler and Oscar Wilde. The following year he traveled in Holland, Belgium, Spain, and Portugal, widening his knowledge of art. He joined the circle of *La Revue Blanche* and made many friends, especially the Natanson brothers. At their home he met Vallotton, Bonnard, and Vuillard, whom he greatly admired. He continued his work at a feverish pace, doing oils, posters, humorous sketches for the newspapers, book illustrations, and lithographs. But excessive drinking threatened his health, and in 1899 his mother sent him to recover at a hospital in Neuilly. Three months after he left the hospital, however, he resumed his restless, irregular life. In July, 1901, he had an attack of paralysis and retired to live with his mother in the Château de Malromé in the Gironde, where he died on September 9.

FÉLIX VALLOTTON

Born in Lausanne on December 28, 1865. He received a rigid Calvinist education. At seventeen he attended the Academy Julian in Paris. In 1885 one of his paintings was accepted by the Salon. He was methodical and meticulous about everything he did, and from this period on he listed everything he painted in his *Livre de Raison*. In his youth he made copies of some paintings by Antonello, Leonardo da Vinci, and Dürer. Around 1892 he dedicated himself to wood engravings, continuing this activity, which gave him greater economic security, for some years. He contributed to *La Revue Blanche* and joined the Nabis group.

After his marriage in 1899 he turned to painting, concentrating on still lifes, nudes, and landscapes. His works, which he exhibited in various shows, were the source of great interest and heated arguments. In 1913 he traveled in Italy and in Russia; then, during the First World War, he visited the front lines and did several unsuccessful paintings. He suffered from ill health, depression, and emotional turmoils. The last year of his life, 1925, was one of his most fruitful and he noted sixty-five paintings in his *Livre de Raison*. His last work, a landscape, is dated December 26, two days before his death.

Félix Vallotton also left us many works of literature, including articles, three novels, and several plays.

VINCENT VAN GOGH

Born March 30, 1853 in Groot-Zundert, Holland. He was encouraged by his father, a Protestant minister, to become an art dealer. He worked from 1869 to 1873 in a branch of the Goupil Gallery in The Hague, then in the London branch (1873–1875), and finally in the main gallery in Paris. Although he loved painting, he had a profound dislike of business, so that in 1876 he suddenly gave up his position. But he still did not know what he wanted to do. He read a great deal, often drew sketches and was sometimes overcome by religious crises. He taught languages at Ramsgate, Kent, in England, and then became a lay preacher in Isleworth, near London. He worked in a book shop in Dordrecht, became a theology student in

VAN GOGH *Woman with Cigar*, 1882 (45.5 x 56 cm) Otterlo, The Netherlands, Rijksmuseum Kröller-Müller

Amsterdam, and attended courses on religion in Brussels. Finally, in January, 1879, he was made a lay preacher at the mining district of the Borinage, where he shared the drudgery and privations of the miners. He emerged exhausted from this experience and never quite recovered.

It was also in the Borinage that he decided that painting was his true vocation. He left the Borinage, where he had done some drawings of the mining life, and moved to Brussels, where he studied anatomy and perspective and then he went to his family home in Etten. In December, 1881, he went to The Hague where, with the help of his cousin, Anton Mauve, he had his first serious attempts at painting. After staying in Nuenen with his family (1883–1885) and in Antwerp (1885–1886), he joined his beloved brother, Theo, in Paris. There he attended Cormon's studio, where he met other young men such as Toulouse-

Lautrec and Anquetin and participated in the animated discussions that followed the Impressionist movement. He sided with the Divisionists and those in favor of synthesis, and he met Pissarro, Seurat, Signac, Bernard, and Gauguin. It was to Gauguin that van Gogh felt closest. When he moved to Arles in order to paint, he asked Gauguin to join him. Gauguin arrived on October 20, 1888, and the two months that followed were fruitful for both of them. But their differences of temperament and the continuous arguments frayed van Gogh's nerves, and on December 23 he attempted to attack his friend with a razor. Afterward, in order to punish himself, he cut off his own ear. This was the first of a series of violent attacks that assailed his last years.

In May, 1889, he entered the psychiatric hospital at Saint-Rémy in Provence. After one year he was transferred to Auvers-sur-Oise, where Doctor Gachet (a friend of Pissarro) took care of him. Things seemed to be going better, but only two months later, on a day when hallucinations attacked his mind, he shot himself. Two days later, on July 29, 1890, he died. With him were his brother, Theo, and his friend Gachet.

EDOUARD VUILLARD

Born in Cuiseaux (Saône et Loire) on November 11,

VAN GOGH *Self-Portrait* (Dedicated to Paul Gauguin), 1888 (62 x 52 cm) Cambridge, Massachusetts, Harvard University, Fogg Art Museum, Maurice Wertheim Collection

1868. He moved to Paris with his family in 1877 and formed friendships with Lugné-Poë, Roussel, and Maurice Denis in high school. He later enrolled with Denis at the Beaux-Arts Academy. Soon after, Vuillard, Denis, and Roussel started attending the Academy Julian (1888), where they met Pierre Bonnard, Ibels, Ranson, and Sérusier, with

VUILLARD *Self-Portrait with Sister*, c. 1892 (23 x 16.5 cm) Philadelphia, Philadelphia Museum of Art, Louis E. Stern Collection

whom they created the Nabis group. In 1891, right after the Nabis exhibit at Le Barc de Boutteville Gallery, Vuillard came in contact with critics, poets, musicians, and theater people, and he also met Mallarmé. He exhibited his work in several places and painted some decorative scenes for the homes of his friends—Alexandre Natanson (1894), Dr. Vaquez (1896), Claude Anet (1898). In 1899, Vollard published a splendid series of Vuillard's lithographs called *Paysages et Intérieurs*.

He was by then an accomplished artist and his works were shown at the Independent Artists' shows and at the Salon d'Automne, as well as in private shows. There are no unusual events in the life of this quiet, reserved artist. He left Paris only for short trips to Holland, London, Switzerland, and Italy and spent summers in Brittany, in Normandy, or at the homes of friends. He finished a large decorative work in the Palais de Chaillot in 1937, and he had a retrospective exhibit a year later in the Musée des Decoratifs. He died during the German occupation, at La Baule on June 21, 1940.

List of Illustrations

Translated by Himilce Novas

Permission by S.P.A.D.E.M. by French Reproduction Rights 1970 for the works of:

Odilon Redon, Emile Bernard, Paul Sérusier, Louis Anquetin, Maurice Denis, Felix Vallotton, Aristide Maillol, Édouard Vuillard, Ker-Xavier Roussel

Permission by A.D.A.G.P. by French Reproduction Rights 1970 for the works of:

Alphonse Marie Mucha

Permission by S.P.A.D.E.M.-A.D.A.G.P. by French Reproduction Rights 1970 for the works of:

Pierre Bonnard.

Printed in Italy by A. Mondadori - Verona